HYECHONG CHUNG took her MA in Psychology of Education
at Sookmyeng Women's University, Seoul before becoming head teacher
at an infant school in Seoul. She has lived in England for eight years
and teaches at the North London Korean School. The thing she enjoys
most about living in London is indulging herself reading
all the books she wants.

PRODEEPTA DAS is an author and photographer whose pictures
have been published in over 20 children's books. His previous books for
Frances Lincoln include *I is for India, Geeta's Day, Prita Goes to India,
Kamal Goes to Trinidad, B is for Bangladesh, P is for Pakistan,
P is for Poland, R is for Russia, S is for South Africa, T is for Turkey,*
and, with Benjamin Zephaniah, *We are Britain!* and *J is for Jamaica.*

For my loving family in the UK and my dear mother – H.C.

*For Jin Kyu, Kim Byeong Sou and the children
of GuNam Elementary School* – P.D.

K is for Korea copyright © Frances Lincoln Limited 2008
Text copyright © Hyechong Chung 2008
Photographs copyright © Prodeepta Das 2008

First published in Great Britain and in the USA in 2008 by
Frances Lincoln Children's Books, 4 Torriano Mews,
Torriano Avenue, London NW5 2RZ
www.franceslincoln.com

First paperback published in Great Britain in 2010

The publishers would like to acknowledge Ifeoma Onyefulu as
the originator of the idea on which this book is based. Ifeoma Onyefulu is
the author and photographer of *A is for Africa*.

A catalogue record for this book is available from the British Library.

ISBN: 978-1-84780-133-3

Set in Hiroshige

Printed in Dongguan, Guangdong, China by Toppan Leefung in November 2009

1 3 5 7 9 8 6 4 2

Author's Note

Korea is a country at the eastern end of the great continent of Asia. Its landscape ranges from high mountains to deep rivers, and its history goes back five thousand years. After the Second World War, Korea was split into two parts, North and South – yet we Koreans are still one ethnic family. We all speak the same language, Hangul, we wear traditional Korean dress called *hanbok*, we live in Korean houses known as *hanok*; and we eat *kimchi* with every meal. We are proud to be Korean. Over the past few decades South Korea's economy has prospered, fuelled by the increasing export of electronics, cars and ships. Seoul, where I come from, is a dynamic and vibrant metropolis. Each time I visit Korea, I am touched by everyone's courtesy and eagerness to help.

정혜영

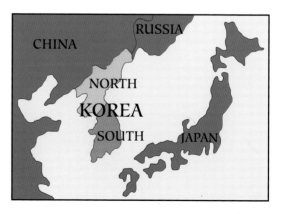

K is for Korea

Hyechong Chung
Prodeepta Das

F

FRANCES LINCOLN
CHILDREN'S BOOKS

 a is for Arirang, folk songs we all love to sing. Our ancestors used to sing them when they were crossing the steep mountain passes of Korea. The most well-known arirang is a bit sad, but there are lots of happy ones too!

Bb

is for Buchaechum, a spectacular fan dance. Young women wearing traditional dress dance and spin, fluttering brightly-coloured fans. They look like flowers in full bloom.

 **C** is for Chuseok, our harvest festival, which takes place in September or October. Families come together for a ceremony of thanksgiving to their ancestors, and a visit to their tombs. Children receive new clothes and presents, fathers enjoy a relaxing week's holiday and mothers are kept busy cooking *songpyen* – rice cakes – and other special dishes.

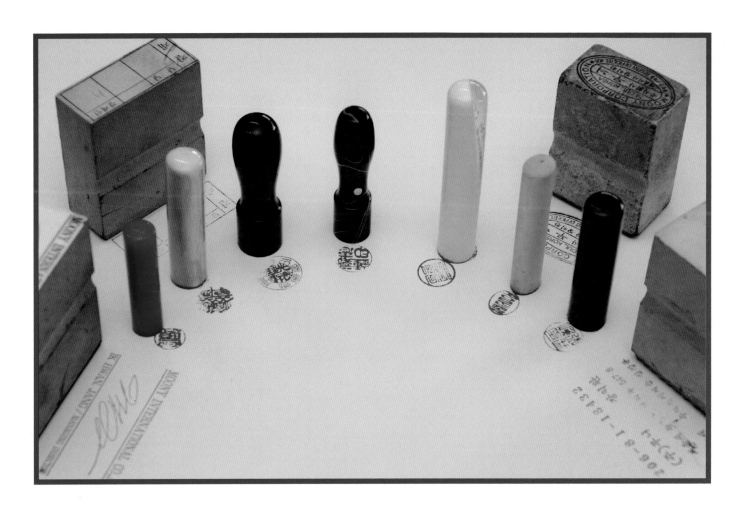

 **D d** is for Dojang, the seal used on official documents. Each seal is made by engraving a person's name on the bottom of a piece of wood or ivory. Then we stamp the seal on official documents, using red ink, to prove that person's identity. We always keep our dojang hidden away in a secret place for safety.

 **e** is for the Emille Bell, a national treasure. This copper bell is the largest in all Korea and has the finest sound. A thousand Buddhist signs and letters are inscribed on the outside of the bell, and people say that when you strike the sign of the lotus, it makes a perfect sound!

F f

is for the Four Seasons. Forsythia greets children in the spring, at the start of a new school year. Summer comes in June, bringing the monsoon – it is hot and humid then, but crops need monsoon rain to grow. Autumn is the best season of all, because everything looks so colourful when the leaves turn yellow and red. Winter, with its frost and heavy snow, is our school holiday time.

G g

is for Ggachi, meaning 'magpie'. It is our national bird and we see it everywhere in the trees. We believe that the ggachi brings good news if we see or hear one singing early in the morning.

Hh

is for Hanbok, our traditional Korean dress, woven from cotton or silk and dyed in vibrant colours. Long ago, every man, woman and child wore hanbok every day. As western clothes become more popular, hanbok is worn only for special occasions such as the New Year, Chuseok and family celebrations.

 **i** is for Ink, used for doing calligraphy – beautiful handwriting. Long ago, every scholar was expected to be a calligrapher, but now people do it as a hobby. You need a brush, black chalk, stone and fine paper – often called 'the scholar's friends'. Fine calligraphy is often hung on the wall like a painting.

 is for Jeol – bowing low to show respect for elderly people or for our ancestors. When a younger person visits an older man or woman, the younger person does jeol to them. We also do jeol at religious rituals and celebrations. There are different jeols for men and for women.

K k is for Korea, a peninsula at the far eastern end of Asia. Much of the land is covered by mountains. Since 1951 Korea has been divided into the democratic South and the communist North, but we all speak the Korean language which has its own alphabet, Hangul. Our two main religions are Buddhism and Christianity.

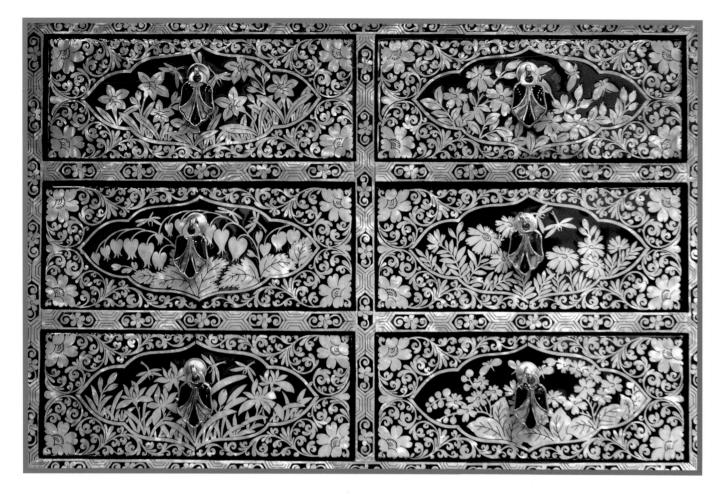

 **l** is for Lacquerware – carved wood inlaid with shiny mother-of-pearl and coated with lacquer. It takes a long time to produce because the inlay decoration often has thirty coats of mother-of-pearl. The lacquer itself is collected from trees once a year and takes a long time to prepare. Each year in October we hold a great lacquerware festival.

Mm

is for Mugungwha, the rose of Sharon. The rosy pink and white flowers start flowering in the spring and go on blooming until autumn. We love Mugunghwa because the flowers seem to smile at us when they bloom.

 **n** is for Namdaemun, the main landmark of Korea's capital city Seoul. Centuries ago it used to be the south gate of Seoul, but now that Seoul has grown in size, it stands in the centre of the city as our national treasure. Namdaemun is surrounded by tall buildings and a famous market.

Oo is for Ondol, our traditional heating system. The ground floor of Korean homes is made of stone and clay, and we burn wood underneath. On cold days we sit on the warm floor eating sweet baked potatoes and listening to our grandparents telling stories.

Pp

is for Pottery, made from fine clay fired at a high temperature. We make big brown pots for storing food as well as pretty tea-cups and priceless porcelain vases. The most beautiful pottery is Koryeo Cheongja, which has delicate designs of clouds and trees.

Qq

is for the Quays of Busan and Incheon, where ships are loaded with electronic goods and cars bound for foreign countries. The roads leading to these ports are always packed with big lorries.

R r is for Rice. Koreans serve boiled rice at every meal as part of the main course. Rice is also the main ingredient in rainbow-coloured rice cakes, crunchy snacks and sweet drinks. *Noorungji*, a crunchy rice scraped from the bottom of the cooking pot, is a traditional Korean snack, and everyone likes to drink noorungji boiled with water at the end of their meal.

S is for Samulnori – percussion music played on four instruments. Each instrument makes a weather noise: a hand-held gong makes the sound of thunder, a large gong makes the wind, a drum makes the moving clouds and an hour-glass-shaped drum makes rain. The musicians dance as they play, shaking their heads and jumping sideways in a circle – which often makes the audience jump too!

 **t** is for Taekwondo, our national martial art and an official sport at the Olympic Games. It is full of high-speed, whirring kicks and powerful hand-strikes which people use to defend themselves. Taekwondo focuses not just on physical strength but also on discipline and respect for others.

**u**

is for Underground, the main form of
transport in crowded cities such as Seoul.
It is the fastest way to get around.
Each busy underground platform has
a push-man who squashes people into
compartments during the rush hour!

**v**

is for Vegetables, growing everywhere in
fields, on mountainsides and in
greenhouses. Our supermarkets and
roadside stalls overflow with vegetables –
because in Korea we eat more vegetables
than meat. In November we are kept
busy washing, salting and seasoning
cabbages and radishes to preserve them
for the cold winter ahead.

w

is for White, the nation's favourite colour. A long time ago, our ancestors wore clothes made from raw cotton which eventually turned white after lots of washings. So Koreans are sometimes called 'the white-clad people'.

 X is for Extra Special Box. Boys keep their marbles in it. Girls use it to store their sparkling accessories. When a woman marries, she receives wedding presents of jewellery in a special wooden box called *ham*.

Yy

is for Yunnori, our favourite family game. Each member of the two teams takes turns to throw the *yut* – four wooden sticks, each with one flat side and one round side – high in the air. The score of flats and rounds is kept with tokens on a square game-board, and the team whose four tokens get back to the starting point first wins the game. Grown-ups enjoy playing yunnori even more than children!

 **z** is for Zing, a type of gong. When the round brass zing is hit using a stick with a cloth-covered end, the low sound lasts for a long time. Farmers sound the zing at harvest festivals and Buddhist monks use it in the temples as part of their traditional ceremonies.

MORE TITLES IN THE WORLD ALPHABET SERIES FROM
FRANCES LINCOLN CHILDREN'S BOOKS

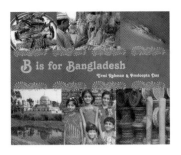

B is for Bangladesh
Urmi Rahman
Photographs by Prodeepta Das

From *Dhaka* to *Jamdani*, from *Crocodile* to *Rickshaw*, this photographic alphabet introduces Bangladesh, a young country with an ancient history and centuries of tradition. Rivers feed the rice-fields and sometimes flood the Bay of Bengal. Yet the Bangladeshi people welcome everyone with a smile.

C is for China
Sungwan So

From *Abacus* to *Lantern*, from *Jade* to *Wenzi*, this photographic alphabet introduces the rich culture and natural beauty of China. Sungwan So's colourful images are a tribute to a traditional society whose people have faced challenges of revolution with courage.

B is for Brazil
Maria de Fatima Campos

From *Carnival* to *Guarana*, from *Football* to *Zebu*, here is a celebration of Brazil in all its cultural diversity. Maria de Fatima Campos illustrates the contrasts between city and rainforest and the vibrant world of Brazilian children.

Frances Lincoln titles are available from all good bookshops.
You can also buy books and find out more about your favourite titles, authors and illustrators on our website: www.franceslincoln.com